The Secrets of the Self

(Asrár-i Khudí)

A PHILOSOPHICAL POEM

By

Muhammad Iqbal

SANAGE
PUBLISHING HOUSE

Paperback: 978-939411240-7

Printed by: Manipal Technologies Limited, Manipal

Sanage Publishing House LLP
Mumbai, India

sanagepublishing@gmail.com

Sir Muhammad Iqbal (9 November 1877 - 21 April 1938), was a South Asian Muslim writer, philosopher, and politician, whose poetry in the Urdu language is considered among the greatest of the twentieth century. He is commonly referred to by the honorific Allama.

CONTENTS

I am born in the world as a new sun,
I have not learned the ways and fashions of the sky:
Not yet have the stars fled before my splendour,
Not yet is my quicksilver astir.
Untouched is the sea by my dancing rays,
Untouched are the mountains by my crimson hue.
The eye of existence is not familiar with me.

I rise trembling, afraid to show myself.
From the East my dawn arrived and routed Night, A fresh dew settled on the rose of the world. I am waiting for the votaries that rise at dawn:
Oh, happy they who shall worship my fire!
I have no need of the ear of To-day,
I am the voice of the poet of To-morrow.

My own age does not understand my deep meanings,
My Joseph is not for this market.
I despair of my old companions,
My Sinai burns for sake of the Moses who is coming.
Their sea is silent, like dew,
But my dew is storm-ridden, like the ocean.
My song is of another world than theirs:
This bell calls other travellers to take the road.
How many a poet after his death?
Opened our eyes when his own were closed,
And journeyed forth again from nothingness
When roses blossomed o'er the earth of his grave!
Albeit caravans have passed through this desert,
They passed, as a camel steps, with little sound.

But I am a lover: loud crying is my faith:
The clamour of Judgement Day is one of my minions.
My song exceeds the range of the chord,
Yet I do not fear that my lute will break.
'Twere better for the waterdrop not to know my torrent,

Whose fury should rather madden the sea.

No river will contain my Omán:[2]
My flood requires whole seas to hold it.
Unless the bud expand into a bed of roses,
It is unworthy of my spring-cloud's bounty.
Lightnings slumber within my soul,

I sweep over mountain and plain.
Wrestle with my sea if thou art a plain.
Receive my lightning if thou art a Sinai.
The Fountain of Life hath been given me to drink,
I have been made an adept of the mystery of Life.
The speck of dust was vitalised by my burning song: It un
folded wings and became a firefly.
No one hath told the secret which I will tell
Or threaded a pearl of thought like mine.
Come, if thou would'st know the secret of everlasting life!
Come, if thou would'st win both earth and heaven!
The old Guru of the Sky taught me this lore,
I cannot hide it from my comrades.
O Saki! arise and pour wine into the cup,
Clear the vexation of Time from my heart!

The sparkling liquor that flows from Zemzem[3]
Were it a beggar, a king would pay homage to it?
It makes thought more sober and wise,
It makes the keen eye keener,
It gives to a straw the weight of a mountain, And to foxes the strength
of lions. It causes dust to soar to the Pleiades
And a drop of water swell to the breadth of the sea.
It turns silence into the din of Judgement Day,

---

[2] The Sea of Oman is a name given by the Arabs to the Persian Gulf.
[3] The holy well at Mecca.

It makes the foot of the partridge red with blood of the hawk.
rise and pour pure wine into my cup,
Pour moonbeams into the dark night of my thought,

That I may lead home the wanderer
And imbue the idle looker-on with restless impatience;
And advance hotly on a new quest
And become known as the champion of a new spirit; A
nd be to people of insight as the pupil to the eye,

And sink into the ear of the world, like a voice.
And exalt the worth of Poesy
And sprinkle the dry herbs with my tears.
Inspired by the genius of the Master of Rúm,[4]
I rehearse the sealed book of secret lore.
His soul is the source of the flames,
I am but as the spark that gleams for a moment.

His burning candle consumed me, the moth.
His wine overwhelmed my goblet.
The Master of Rúm transmuted my earth to gold
And clothed my barren dust with beauty.
The grain of sand set forth from the desert,
That it might win the radiance of the sun.
I am a wave, and I will come to rest in his sea,
That I may make the glistening pearl mine own.
I who am drunken with the wine of his song
Will draw life from the breath of his words.

'Twas night: my heart would fain lament,
The. silence was filled with my cries to God.
I was complaining of the sorrows of the world
And bewailing the emptiness of my cup.

---

[4] Jaláluddín Rúmí, the greatest mystical poet of Persia (a.d. 1207-1273). Most of his life was passed at Iconium in Galatia, for which reason he is generally known as "Rúmí," *i.e.* " the Anatolian."

At last mine eye could endure no more,
Broken with fatigue it went to sleep.
There appeared the Master, formed in the mould of Truth,
Who wrote the Koran of Persia.[5]
He said, "O frenzied lover,
Take a draught of love's pure wine.
Strike the chords of thine heart and rouse a tumultuous strain,
Dash thine head against the cupping-glass and thine eye against the lancet!
Make thy laughter the source of a hundred sighs,
Make the hearts of men bleed with thy tears!

How long wilt thou be silent, like a bud?
Sell thy fragrance cheap, like the rose!

Tongue-tied, thou art in pain:
Cast thyself upon the fire, like rue![6]
Like the bell, break silence at last, a
nd from every limb Utter forth a lamentation!
Thou art fire: fill the world with thy glow!
Make others burn with thy burning!
Proclaim the secrets of the old wine-seller,[7]
Be thou a surge of wine, and the crystal cup thy robe!
Shatter the mirror of fear,
Break the bottles in the bazaar!
Like the reed-flute, bring a message from the reeds;
Give to Majnún a message from Lailá![8]
Create a new style for thy song,
Enrich the feast with thy piercing strains!
Up and re-inspire every living soul!
Say 'Arise!' and by that word quicken the living!

---

[5] This refers to the famous *Masnaví* of Jaláluddín Rúmí.
[6] Rue-seed, which is burned for the purpose of fumigation, crackles in the fire.
[7] "Wine " signifies the mysteries of divine love.
[8] Majnún is the Orlando Furioso of Arabia.

Up, and set thy feet on another path.
Put aside the passionate melancholy of old!
Become familiar with the delight of singing.
O bell of the caravan, awake!"

At these words my bosom was enkindled
And swelled with emotion like the flute.
I rose like music from the string
To prepare a Paradise for the ear.
I unveiled the mystery of the. Self
And disclosed its wondrous secret.

My being was as an unfinished statue,
Uncomely, worthless, good for nothing.
Love chiselled me: I became a man
And gained knowledge of the nature of the universe.

I have seen the movement of the sinews of the sky,
And the blood coursing in the veins of the moon.
Many a night I wept for Man's sake
That I might tear the veil from Life's mysteries,
And extract the secret of Life's constitution
From the laboratory of phenomena.

I who give beauty to this night, like the moon,

Am as dust in devotion to the pure Faith (Islam)
A Faith renowned in hill and dale,
Which kindles in men's hearts a flame of undying song:
It sowed an atom and reaped a sun,
It harvested a hundred poets like Rumi and Attar.
I am a sigh: I will mount to the heavens.
I am a breath, yet am I sprung of fire.

Driven onward by high thoughts, my
pen Cast abroad the secret of this veil,

That the drop may become co-equal with the sea
And the grain of sand grow into a Sahara.
Poetising is not the aim of this *masnaví*,
Beauty-worshipping and lovemaking is not its aim.
I am of India: Persian is not my native tongue;
I am like the crescent moon: my cup is not full.
Do not seek from me charm of style in exposition,
Do not seek from me Khánsár and Isfahan.[9]
Although the language of Hind is sweet as sugar,
Yet sweeter is the fashion of Persian speech.

My mind was enchanted by its loveliness,
My pen became as a twig of the Burning Bush.
ecause of the loftiness of my thoughts,
persian alone is suitable to them.
O Reader do not find fault with the wine-cup
But consider attentively the taste of the wine.

[9] Khánsár, which lies about a hundred miles north- west of Isfahan, was the birthplace of several Persian poets.

1. Showing That The System Of The Universe Originates In The Self...

SHOWING THAT THE SYSTEM OF THE UNIVERSE ORIGINATES IN THE SELF, AND THAT THE CONTINUATION OF THE LIFE OF ALL INDIVIDUALS DEPENDS ON STRENGTHENING THE SELF

The form of existence is an effect of the Self,
Whatsoever thou seest is a secret of the Self.
When the Self awoke to consciousness,
It revealed the universe of Thought.
A hundred worlds are hidden in its essence:
Self-affirmation brings Not-self to light.
By the Self the seed of hostility is sown in the world:
It imagines itself to be other than itself.

It makes from itself the forms of others
In order to multiply the pleasure of strife.
It is slaying by the strength of its arm
That it may become conscious of its own strength.
Its self-deceptions are the essence of Life.
Like the rose, it lives by bathing itself in blood.
For the sake of a single rose, it destroys a hundred rose-gardens

And makes a hundred lamentations in quest of a single melody.
For one sky it produces a hundred new moons,
And for one word a hundred discourses.
he excuse for this wastefulness and cruelty
Is the shaping and perfecting of spiritual beauty.

The loveliness of Shírín justifies the anguish
of Farhád,[1] The fragrant navel justifies a hundred musk-
deer. 'Tis the fate of moths to consume in flame:
The suffering of moths is justified by the candle.

The pencil of the Self limned a hundred todays
In order to achieve the dawn of a single morrow.
Its flames burned a hundred Abrahams[2]
That the lamp of one Mohammed might be lighted.
Subject, object, means, and causes
They all exist for the purpose of action.

The Self rises, kindles, falls, glows, breathes,
Burns, shines, walks, and flies.
The spaciousness of Time is its arena,
Heaven is a billow of the dust on its road.
From its rose-planting the world abounds in roses.
Night is born of its sleep, day springs from its waking.
It divided its flame into sparks
And taught the understanding to worship particulars.
It dissolved itself and created the atoms,
It was scattered for a little while and created the sands.
Then it wearied of dispersion
And by re-uniting itself it became the mountains.
'Tis the nature of the Self to manifest itself:

---

[1] Shírín was loved by the Persian emperor Khusrau Parwíz. Farhád fell in love with her and cast himself down a precipice on hearing a false rumour of her death.

[2] Abraham is said to have been cast on a burning pile by order of Nimrod and miraculously preserved from harm.

In every atom slumbers the might of the Self.

Power that is unexpressed and inert
Chains the faculties which lead to action.
Inasmuch as the life of the universe
comes from the strength of the Self,
Life is in proportion to this strength.
When a drop of water gets the Self's lesson by heart,
It makes its worthless existence a pearl.
Wine is formless because it's self is weak;
It receives a form by favour of the cup.
Although the cup of wine assumes a form,
It is indebted to us for its motion.
When the mountain loses it's self, it turns into sands

And complains that the sea surges over it.
But the wave, so long as it remains a wave in the sea's
bosom, Makes itself a rider on the sea's back.

Light has been a beggar since the eye first rolled
And moved to and fro in search of beauty; But forasmuch as the grass
found a means of growth in its self,
Its aspiration clove the breast of the garden.
The candle too concatenated itself
And built itself out of atoms.
Then it made a practice of melting
itself away and fled from its self
Until at last it trickled down from its own eye, like tears.
If the bezel had been more self-secure by nature,
It would not have suffered wounds,
But since it derives its value from the superscription,
Its shoulder is galled by the burden of another's name.
Because the earth is firmly based on self-existence,

The captive moon goes round it perpetually.
The being of the sun is stronger than that of the earth:
Therefore, is the earth bewitched by the sun's eye.
The glory of the plane fixes our gaze,
The mountains are enriched by its majesty:
Its raiment is woven of fire,
Its origin is one self-assertive seed.
When Life gathers strength from the Self,
The river of Life expands into an ocean.

2. Showing That The Life Of The Self Comes From Forming Desires And Bringing Them To Birth

SHOWING THAT THE LIFE OF THE SELF COMES FROM FORMING DESIRES AND BRINGING THEM TO BIRTH

Life is preserved by purpose:
Because of the goal its caravan-bell tinkles.
Life is latent in seeking,
Its origin is hidden in desire.
Keep desire alive in thy heart,
Lest thy little dust become a tomb.
Desire is the soul of this world of hue and scent,
The nature of everything is faithful to desire.
Desire sets the heart dancing in the breast,

And by its glow the breast is made bright as a mirror.
It gives to earth the power of soaring, It is a Khizr to

the Moses of perception.[1] From the flame of desire
the heart takes life, And when it takes life, all dies
that is not true. When it refrains from forming
wishes, Its pinion breaks and it cannot soar. Desire is
an emotion of the Self:

It is a restless wave of the Self's sea.
Desire is a noose for hunting ideals,
A binder of the book of deeds.
Negation of desire is death to the living,
Even as absence of burning extinguishes the flame.
What is the source of our wakeful eye?
Our delight in seeing hath taken visible shape.

The partridge's leg is derived from the elegance of its gait,
The nightingale's beak from its endeavour to sing.
Away from the reed-bed, the reed became happy:
The music was released from its prison.[2]
Why does the mind strive after new discoveries and scale the heavens?
Knowest thou what works this miracle?
'Tis desire that enriches Life,
And the intellect is a child of its womb.
What are social organisation, customs, and laws?
What is the secret of the novelties of science?
A desire which broke through by its own strength
And burst forth from the heart and took shape.

Nose, hand, brain, eye, and ear,
Thought, imagination, feeling, memory, and understanding
All these are weapons devised for self-preservation By him
that rides into the battle of Life.

---

[1] Cf. Koran, ch. 18, vv. 64-80. Khizr represents the mystic seer whose actions are misjudged by persons of less insight.

[2] *I.e.* the reed was made into a flute.

The object of science and art is not knowledge,
The object of the garden is not the bud and the flower.
Science is an instrument for the preservation of Life,
Science is a means of establishing the Self.
Science and art are servants of Life,
Slaves born and bred in its house.
Rise, O thou who art strange to Life's mystery,
Rise intoxicated with the wine of an ideal!
If thou art an ideal, thou wilt shine as the dawn

And be to all else as a blazing fire.
If thou art an ideal, thou art higher than
Heaven Winning, captivating, enchanting men's
hearts; A destroyer of ancient falsehood,
Fraught with turmoil, an embodiment of the Last Day.

We live by forming ideals,
We glow with the sunbeams of desire!

3. Showing That The Self Is Strengthened By Love

SHOWING THAT THE SELF IS STRENGTHENED BY LOVE

The luminous point whose name is the Self
Is the life-spark beneath our dust.
By Love it is made more lasting,
More living, more burning, more glowing.
From Love proceeds the radiance of its being
And the development of its unknown possibilities.
Its nature gathers fire from Love,
Love instructs it to illumine the world.

Love fears neither sword nor dagger,
Love is not born of water and air and earth.
Love makes peace and war in the world,
The Fountain of Life is Love's flashing sword.
The hardest rocks are shivered by Love's glance:
Love of God at last becomes wholly God.
Learn thou to love, and seek to be loved:
Seek an eye like Noah's, a heart like Job's!

Transmute thy handful of earth into gold,
Kiss the threshold of a Perfect Man! [1]
Like Rúmí, light thy candle
And burn Rúm in the fire of Tabríz![2]

There is a beloved hidden within thine heart:
I will show him to thee if thou hast eyes to see.
His lovers are fairer than the fair,
Sweeter and comelier and more beloved.
By love of him the heart is made strong, A
nd earth rubs shoulders with the Pleiades.
The soil of Najd was quickened by his grace

And fell into a rapture and rose to the skies.[3]
In the Moslem's heart is the home of Mohammed, All our glory is from the name of Mohammed. Sinai is but an eddy of the dust of his house,
The sanctuary of the Ka'ba is his dwelling-place.

Eternity is less than a moment of his time,
Eternity receives increase from his essence.
He slept on a mat of rushes,
But the crown of Chosroes was under his people's feet.
He chose the nightly solitude of Mount Hira,
And he founded a state and laws and government.
He passed many a night with sleepless eyes
In order that the Moslems might sleep on the throne of Persia. In the hour of battle, iron was melted by his sword; In the hour of prayer, tears fell like rain from his eye.
When he was called to aid, his sword answered "Amen"
And extirpated the race of kings.
He instituted new laws in the world,

---

[1] A prophet or saint.
[2] See note on l. 95. Tabríz is an allusion to Shams-i Tabríz, the spiritual director of Jalálu'ddín Rúmí..
[3] Najd, the Highlands of Arabia, is celebrated in love-romance. I need only mention Laud and Majnún.

He brought the empires of antiquity to an end.
With the key of religion he opened the door of this world:
The womb of the world never bore his like.
In his sight high and low were one,
He sat with his slave at one table.
The daughter of the chieftain of Tai
was taken prisoner in battle[4]
And brought into that exalted presence;
Her feet in chains, unveiled,
And her neck bowed with shame.
When the Prophet saw that the poor girl had no
veil, He covered her face with his own veil.
We are more naked than that lady of Tai,
We are unveiled before the nations of the world.

In him is our trust on the Day of Judgement,
And in this world too he is our protector.
Both his favour and his wrath are entirely a mercy:
That is a mercy to his friends and this to his foes.
He opened the gates of mercy to his enemies,
He gave to Mecca the message, "No blame shall be laid upon you.
" We who know not the bonds of country
Resemble sight, which is one though it be the light of two eyes.
We belong to the Hijáz and China and Persia, Yet we are the
dew of one smiling dawn.
We are all under the spell of the eye of the cupbearer from Mecca,
We are united as wine and cup.

He burnt clean away distinctions of lineage,
His fire consumed this trash and rubble.
We are like a rose with many petals but with one perfume:
He is the soul of this society, and he is one.
We were the secret concealed in his heart:

---

[4] Her father, Hátim of Tai, is proverbial in the East for his hospitality.

He spoke out fearlessly, and we were revealed.
The song of love for him fills my silent reed,
A hundred notes throb in my bosom.
How shall I tell what devotion he inspires?
A block of dry wood wept at parting from him.[5]
The Moslem's being is where he manifests his glory:
Many a Sinai springs from the dust on his path.

My image was created by his mirror,
My dawn rises from the sun of his breast.
My repose is a perpetual fever,
My evening hotter than the morning of Judgement Day:[6]
He is the April cloud and I his garden,
My vine is bedewed with his rain.
I sowed mine eye in the field of Love
And reaped a harvest of delight.

"The soil of Medina is sweeter than both worlds:
Oh, happy the town where dwells the Beloved!"[7]
I am lost in admiration of the style of Mullá Jámí:
His verse and prose are a remedy for my immaturity.
He has written poetry overflowing with beautiful ideas

And has threaded pearls in praise of the Master
"Mohammed is the preface to the book of the universe:
All the world are slaves, and he is the Master."
From the wine of Love spring many qualities:
Amongst the attributes of Love is blind devotion.
The saint of Bistám, who in devotion was unique,
Abstained from eating a watermelon.[8]
Be a lover constant in devotion to thy beloved,

---

[5] The story of the pulpit that wept when Mohammed descended from it occurs, I think, in the *Masnaví*.
[6] When, according to Mohammedan belief, the sun will rise in the west.
[7] A quotation from the Masnaví. The Prophet was buried at Medina.
[8] Báyazíd of Bistám died in a.d. 875. He refused to eat a watermelon, saying he had no assurance that the Prophet had ever tasted that fruit.

That thou mayst cast thy noose and capture God.
Sojourn for a while on the Hirá of the heart,[9]

Abandon self and flee to God.
Strengthened by God, return to thy self
And break the heads of the Lát and Uzzá of
sensuality.[10] By the might of Love evoke an army,
Reveal thyself on the Fárán of Love,[11]
That the Lord of the Ka'ba may show thee favour
And interpret to thee the text, "Lo, I will appoint a vicegerent on the earth." [12]

---

[9] Mohammed used to retire to a cave on Mount Hirá, near Mecca, for the purpose of solitary meditation and other ascetic observances.

[10] Lát and Uzzá were goddesses worshipped by the heathen Arabs.

[11] Fárán, name of a mountain in the neighbourhood of Mecca.

[12] Koran, ch. 2, v. 28. In these words, which were addressed to the angels, God foretold the creation of Adam.

4. Showing That The Self Is Weakened By Asking

SHOWING THAT THE SELF IS WEAKENED BY ASKING

O thou who hast gathered taxes from lions,
Thy need hath caused thee to become a fox in disposition.
Thy maladies are the result of indigence:
This disease is the source of thy pain.
It is robbing thine high thoughts of their dignity
And putting out the light of thy noble imagination.
Quaff rosy wine from the jar of existence!

Snatch thy money from the purse of Time!
Like Omar, come down from thy camel![1]
Beware of incurring obligations, beware!
How long wilt thou sue for office
And ride like children on a woman's back?
A nature that fixes its gaze on the sky
Becomes debased by receiving benefits.
By asking, poverty is made more abject.

---

[1] The Caliph Omar was a man of simple habits and self-reliant character.

By begging, the beggar is made poorer.
Asking disintegrates the Self
And deprives of illumination the Sinai-bush of the Self.
Do not scatter thy handful of dust.
Like the moon, scrape food from thine own side!
Albeit thou art poor and wretched

And overwhelmed by affliction,
Seek not thy daily bread from the bounty of another,
Seek not waves of water from the fountain of the sun,
Lest thou be put to shame before the Prophet
On the Day when every soul shall be stricken with fear.
The moon gets sustenance from the table of the sun
And bears the brand of his bounty on her heart.
Pray God for courage! Wrestle with Fortune!
Do not sully the honour of the pure religion!
He who swept the rubbish of idols out of the Ka'ba
Said that God loves a man that earns his living.
Woe to him that accepts bounty from another's table

And lets his neck be bent with benefits!
He hath consumed himself with the lightning of the favours bestowed on him,
He hath sold his honour for a paltry coin.
Happy the man who thirsting in the sun
Does not crave of Khizr a cup of water![2]
His brow is not moist with the shame of beggary.
He is a man still, not a piece of clay.
That noble youth walks under heaven
With his head erect like the pine.
Are his hands empty? The more is he master of himself.
Do his fortunes languish? The more alert is he.
The beggar's wallet is like a boat tossing in waves of fire.

---

[2] Khizr is supposed to have drunk of the Fountain of Life.

Sweet is a little dew gathered by one's own hand.
Be a man of honour, and like the bubble
Keep thy cup inverted even in the midst of the sea![3]

[3] The bubble is compared to an inverted cup, which of course receives nothing.

5. Showing That When The Self Is Strengthened By Love It Gains Dominion...

SHOWING THAT WHEN THE SELF IS STRENGTHENED BY LOVE IT GAINS DOMINION OVER THE OUTWARD AND INWARD FORCES OF THE UNIVERSE

When the Self is made strong by Love
Its power rules the whole world.
The Heavenly Sage who adorned the sky with stars
Plucked these buds from the bough of the Self.
Its hand becomes God's hand,
The moon is split by its fingers.
It is the arbitrator in all the quarrels of the world,
Its command is obeyed by Darius and Jamshíd.

I will tell thee a story of Bú Ali,[1]
Whose name is renowned in India,
Him who sang of the ancient rose-garden

[1] Sheikh Sharafu'ddín of Pánípat, who is better known as Bú Ali Qalandar, was a great saint. He died about a.d. 1325.

And discoursed to us about the lovely rose:
The air of his fluttering skirt
Made a Paradise of this fire-born country.
His young disciple went one day to the bazaar,
The wine of Bú Ali's discourse had turned his head.
The governor of the city was coming along on horseback,
His servant and staff-bearer rode beside him.
The forerunner shouted, "O senseless one,
Do not get in the way of the governor's escort!"

But the dervish walked on with drooping head,
Sunk in the sea of his own thoughts.
The staff-bearer, drunken with pride,
Broke his staff on the head of the dervish,

Who stepped painfully out of the governor's way,
Sad and sorry, with a heavy heart.
He came to Bú Ali and complained
And released the tears from his eyes.
Like lightning that falls on mountains,
The Sheikh poured forth a fiery torrent of speech.
He let loose from his soul a strange fire,
He gave an order to his secretary:
Take thy pen and write a letter
From a dervish to a sultan!
Say, 'Thy governor has broken my servant's head;
He has cast burning coals on his own life.

Arrest this wicked governor,
Or else I will bestow thy kingdom on another.'
" The letter of the saint who had access to God
Caused the monarch to tremble in every limb.
His body was filled with aches,
He grew as pale as the evening sun.
He sought out a handcuff for the governor

And entreated Bú Ali to pardon this offence.
Khusrau, the sweet-voiced eloquent poet,[2]
Whose harmonies flow from the creative mind
And whose genius hath the soft brilliance of moonlight,
Was chosen to be the king's ambassador.

When he entered Bú Ali's presence and played his lute,
His song melted the fakir's soul like glass.
One strain of poesy bought the grace
Of a majesty that was firm as a mountain.
Do not wound the hearts of dervishes,
Do not throw thyself into burning fire!

[2] Amír Khusrau of Delhi, the most celebrated of the Persian poets of India.

6. A Tale Of Which The Moral Is That Negation Of The Self Is A Doctrine...

A TALE OF WHICH THE MORAL IS THAT NEGATION OF THE SELF IS A DOCTRINE INVENTED BY THE SUBJECT RACES OF MANKIND IN ORDER THAT BY THIS MEANS THEY MAY SAP AND WEAKEN THE CHARACTER OF THEIR RULERS

Hast, thou heard that in the time of old
The sheep dwelling in a certain pasture
So increased and multiplied
That they feared no enemy?
At last, from the malice of Fate,
Their breasts were smitten by a shaft of calamity.
The tigers sprang forth from the jungle
And rushed upon the sheepfold.

Conquest and dominion are signs of strength,
Victory is the manifestation of strength.
Those fierce tigers beat the drum of sovereignty,

They deprived the sheep of freedom.
Forasmuch as tigers must have their prey,
That meadow was crimsoned with the blood of the sheep.
One of the sheep, which was clever and acute,
Old in years, cunning as a weather-beaten wolf,
Being grieved at the fate of his fellows
And sorely vexed by the violence of the tigers,
Made complaint of the course of, Destiny
And sought by craft to restore his fortunes.
The weak man, in order to preserve himself,

Seeks devices from skilled intelligence.
In slavery, for the sake of repelling harm,
The power of scheming becomes quickened,
And when the madness of revenge gains hold,
The mind of the slave meditates rebellion.
"Ours is a hard knot," said this sheep to himself,
"The ocean of our griefs hath no shore.
By force we sheep cannot escape from the tiger:
Our legs are silver, his paws are steel.
'Tis not possible, however much one exhorts and
counsels, To create in a sheep the disposition of a wolf.
But to make the furious tiger a sheep that is possible;
To make him unmindful of his nature that is possible."

He became as a prophet inspired,
And began to preach to the blood-thirsty tigers.
He cried out, "O ye insolent liars,
Who wot not of a day of ill luck that shall continue
for ever![1] I am possessed of spiritual power,
I am an apostle sent by God for the tigers.
I come as a light for the eye that is dark,
I come to establish laws and give commandments.

---

[1] These expressions are borrowed from the Koran.

Repent of your blameworthy deeds!
O plotters of evil, bethink yourselves of good!
Whoso is violent and strong is miserable:
Life's solidity depends on self-denial.
The spirit of the righteous is fed by fodder:
The vegetarian is pleasing unto God.

The sharpness of your teeth brings disgrace upon you
And makes the eye of your perception blind.
Paradise is for the weak alone,
Strength is but a means to perdition.
It is wicked to seek greatness and glory,
Penury is sweeter than princedom.
Lightning does not threaten the corn-seed:
If the seed become a stack, it is unwise.
If you are sensible, you will be a mote of sand,
not a Sahara, So that you may enjoy the sunbeams.

O thou that delightest in the slaughter of sheep,
Slay thy self, and thou wilt have honour!
Life is rendered unstable
By violence, oppression, revenge, and exercise of power.

Though trodden underfoot, the grass grows up time after time
And washes the sleep of death from its eye again and again.
Forget thy self if thou art wise!
If thou dost not forget thy self, thou art mad.
Close thine eyes, close thine ears, close thy lips,[2]
That thy thought may reach the lofty sky!
This pasturage of the world is naught, naught:
O fool, do not torment thyself for a phantom!"
The tiger-tribe was exhausted by hard struggles,
They had set their hearts on enjoyment of luxury.

---

[2] Quoted from the Masnaví.

This soporific advice pleased them,
In their stupidity they swallowed the charm of the sheep.
He that used to make sheep his prey
Now embraced a sheep's religion.
'flee tigers took kindly to a diet of fodder:
At length their tigerish nature was broken.
The fodder blunted their teeth
And put out the awful flashings of their eyes.
By degrees courage ebbed from their breasts,
The sheen departed from the mirror.
That frenzy of uttermost exertion remained not,
That craving after action dwelt in their hearts no more.
They lost the power of ruling and the resolution to be
independent, They lost reputation, prestige, and fortune.
Their paws that were as iron became strengthless;
Their souls died, and their bodies became tombs.
Bodily strength diminished while spiritual fear increased:
Spiritual fear robbed them of courage.
Lack of courage produced a hundred diseases Poverty,
pusillanimity, lowmindedness.
The wakeful tiger was lulled to slumber by the sheep's charm:
He called his decline Moral Culture.

7. To The Effect That Plato, Whose Thought Has Deeply Influenced The Mysticism...

TO THE EFFECT THAT PLATO, WHOSE THOUGHT HAS DEEPLY INFLUENCED THE MYSTICISM AND LITERATURE OF ISLAM, FOLLOWED THE SHEEP'S DOCTRINE, AND THAT WE MUST BE ON OUR GUARD AGAINST HIS THEORIES

Plato, the prime ascetic, and sage,
Was one of that ancient flock of sheep.

His Pegasus went astray in the darkness of
philosophy And galloped over the mountains of
Being. He was so fascinated by the Ideal
That he made head, eye, and ear of no account.
"To die," said he, "is the secret of Life:
The candle is glorified by being put out."
He dominates our thinking,
His cup sends us to sleep and takes the world away from us.
He is a sheep in man's clothing,
The soul of the Sufi bows to his authority.

He soared with his intellect to the highest heaven,
He called the world of phenomena a myth. '
Twas his work to dissolve the structure of Life

And cut the bough of Life's fair tree asunder.
The thought of Plato regarded loss as profit,
His philosophy declared that being is not-being.
His nature drowsed and created a dream,
His mind's eye created a mirage.
Since he was without any taste for action,
His soul was enraptured by the non-existent.
He disbelieved in the material universe
And became the creator of invisible Ideas.
Sweet is the world of phenomena to the living spirit,
Dear is the world of Ideas to the dead spirit:
Its gazelles have no grace of movement,
Its partridges are denied the pleasure of walking daintily.

Its dewdrops are unable to quiver,
Its birds have no breath in their breasts,
Its seed does not desire to grow,
Its moths do not know how to flutter.
Our philosopher had no remedy but flight:
He could not endure the noise of this world.
He set his heart on the glow of a quenched flame
And depicted a world steeped in opium.
He spread his wings towards the sky
And never came down to his nest again.
His phantasy is sunk in the jar of heaven:
I know not whether it is the dregs or the bricks. [1]
The peoples were poisoned by his intoxication:
He slumbered and took no delight in deeds.

---

[1] *I.e.* it is worthless in either case. The egg-shaped wine jar is supported by bricks in order to keep it in an upright position.

8. Concerning The True Nature Of Poetry And The Reform Of Islamic Literature

CONCERNING THE TRUE NATURE OF POETRY AND THE REFORM OF ISLAMIC LITERATURE

'Tis the brand of desire makes the blood of man run warm,
By the lamp of desire this dust is enkindled.
By desire Life's cup is brimmed with wine,
So that Life leaps to its feet and marches briskly on.

Life is occupied with conquest alone, And
the one charm for conquest is desire.
Life is the hunter and desire the snare,
Desire is Love's message to Beauty.
Wherefore doth desire swell continuously
The bass and treble of Life's song?
Whatsoever is good and fair and beautiful
Is our guide in the wilderness of seeking.
Its image becomes impressed on thine heart,
It creates desires in thine heart.

Beauty is the creator of desire's springtide;
Desire is nourished by the display of Beauty.
'Tis in the poet's breast that Beauty unveils,
'Tis from his Sinai that Beauty's beams arise.
By his look the fair is made fairer,
Through his enchantments Nature is more beloved.
From his lips the nightingale hath learned her song,
And his rouge hath brightened the cheek of the rose.

'Tis his passion burns in the heart of the moth,
'Tis he that lends glowing hues to love-tales.
Sea and land are hidden within his water and clay,[1]
A hundred new worlds are concealed in his heart.
Ere tulips blossomed in his brain
There was heard no note of joy or grief.
His music breathes o'er us a wonderful enchantment,
His pen draws a mountain with a single hair.
His thoughts dwell with the moon and the stars,
He creates beauty in that which is ugly and strange.
He is a Khizr, and amidst his darkness is the Fountain of Life:[2]

All things that exist are made more living by his tears.
Heavily we go, like raw novices,
Stumbling on the way to the goal.
His nightingale hath played a tune
And laid a plot to beguile us,
That he may lead us into Life's Paradise,
And that Life's bow may become a full circle.
Caravans march at the sound of his bell And
follow the voice of his pipe.
But when his zephyr blows in our gardens,
We stay loitering amongst tulips and roses.
His witchery makes Life develop itself

[1] *I.e.* in his body.
[2] Khizr, according to the legend, discovered the Fountain of Life in the Land of Darkness.

And become self-questioning and impatient.
He invites the whole world to his table.
He lavishes his fire as though it were cheap as air.
Woe to a people that resigns itself to death,

And whose poet turns away from the joy of living!
His mirror shows beauty as ugliness,
His honey leaves a hundred stings in the heart.
His kiss robs the rose of freshness,
He takes away from the nightingale's heart the joy of flying.
Thy sinews are relaxed by his opium,
Thou payest for his song with thy life.
He bereaves the cypress of delight in its beauty,
His cold breath makes a pheasant of the male falcon.
He is a fish, and from the breast upward a man,

Like the Sirens in the ocean.
With his song he enchants the pilot
And casts the ship to the bottom of the sea.
His melodies steal firmness from thine heart,

His magic persuades thee that death is life.
He takes from thy soul the desire of existence,
He extracts from thy mine the blushing ruby.
He dresses gain in the garb of loss,
He makes everything praiseworthy blameful.
He plunges thee in a sea of thought,
He makes thee a stranger to action.
He is sick, and by his words our sickness is increased:
The more his cup goes round, the more sick are they that quaff it.
There are no lightning rains in his April,
His garden is a mirage of colour and perfume.
His beauty hath no dealings with Truth,
There are none but flawed pearls in his sea.
Slumber he deemed sweeter than waking:

Our fire was quenched by his breath.
By the chant of his nightingale the heart was poisoned:
Under his heap of roses lurked a snake.
Beware of his decanter and cup!
Beware of his sparkling wine!
O thou whom his wine hath laid low
And who look'st to his glass for thy rising dawn,
O thou whose heart hath been chilled by his melodies,
Thou hast drunk deadly poison through the ear!
Thy way of life is a proof of thy degeneracy,
The strings of thine instrument are out of tune.
'Tis pampered ease hath made thee so wretched,
A disgrace to Islam throughout the world.
One can bind thee with the vein of a rose,

One can wound thee with a zephyr.
Love hath been put to shame by thy wailing,
His fair picture hath been fouled by thy brush.
Thy ill-usage hath paled his cheek,
Thy coldness hath taken the glow from his fire.
He is heartsick from thy heart-sicknesses,
And enfeebled by thy feebleness's.
His cup is full of childish tears,
His house is furnished with distressful sighs.[3]
He is a drunkard begging at tavern-doors,
Stealing glimpses of beauty from lattices,
Unhappy, melancholy, injured,
Kicked well-nigh to death by the warder;
Wasted like a reed by sorrows,
On his lips a store of complaints against Heaven.
Flattery and spite are the mettle of his
mirror, Helplessness his comrade of old.

---

[3] In this passage the author assails the Persian and Urdu poetry so much in favour with his contemporaries.

A miserable base-born underling
Without worth or hope or object,
Whose lamentations have sucked the marrow from thy
soul And driven off gentle sleep from thy neighbours' eyes.
Alas for a love whose fire is extinct,
A love that was born in the Holy
Place and died in the house of idols!
Oh, if thou hast the coin of poesy in thy
purse, Rub it on the touchstone of Life!
Clear-seeing thought shows the way to action,
As the lightning-flash precedes the thunder.

It behoves thee to meditate well concerning literature,
It behoves thee to go back to the Arabs:
Thou must needs give thine heart to the Salmá of Araby,[4]
That the morn of the Hijáz may blossom
from the night of Kurdistan.[5]
Thou hast gathered roses from the garden of
Persia And seen the springtide of India and Iran:

Now taste a little of the heat of the desert,
Drink the old wine of the date!
Lay thine head for once on its hot breast,
Yield thy body awhile to its scorching wind!
For a long time, thou hast turned about on a bed of silk:

---

[4] Arabic odes usually begin with a prelude in which the poet makes mention of his beloved; and her name is often Salmá. Here "the Salmá of Araby" refers to the Koran and the ideals for which it stands.

[5] It is related that an ignorant Kurd came to some students and besought them to instruct him in the mysteries of Sufism. They told him that he must fasten a rope to the roof of his house, then tie the loose end to his feet and suspend himself, head downwards; and that he must remain in this posture as long as possible, reciting continually some words of gibberish which they taught him. The poor man did not perceive that he was being mocked. He followed their instructions and passed the whole night repeating the words given him. God rewarded his faith and sincerity by granting him illumination, so that he became a saint and could discourse learnedly on the most abstruse matters of mystical theology. Afterwards he used to say, "In the evening I was a Kurd, but the next morning I was an Arab."

Now accustom thyself to rough cotton!
For generations thou hast danced on tulips
And bathed thy cheek in dew, like the rose:
Now throw thyself on the burning sand
And plunge into the fountain of Zemzem!
How long wilt thou fain lament like the nightingale?
How long make thine abode in gardens?
O thou whose auspicious snare would do honour to the
Phoenix, Build a nest on the high mountains,
A nest embosomed in lightning and thunder,
Loftier than eagle's eyrie,
That thou mayst be fit for Life's battle,
That thy body and soul may burn in Life's fire!

9. Showing That The Education Of The Self Has Three Stages...

SHOWING THAT THE EDUCATION OF THE SELF HAS THREE STAGES: OBEDIENCE, SELF-CONTROL, AND DIVINE VICEGERENCY

1. Obedience

Service and toil are traits of the camel,
Patience and perseverance are ways of the camel.
Noiselessly he steps along the sandy track,
He is the ship of those who voyage in the desert.
Every thicket knows the print of his foot:
He eats seldom, sleeps little, and is inured to toil.

He carries rider, baggage, and litter.
He trots on and on to the journey's end, Rejoicing in his speed,
More patient in travel than his rider.
Thou, too, do not refuse the burden of Duty:
So, wilt thou enjoy the best dwelling-place, which is with God.
Endeavour to obey, O heedless one!
Liberty is the fruit of compulsion.
By obedience the man of no worth is made worthy; By disobedience

his fire is turned to ashes.
Whoso would master the sun and stars, Let him make himself a prisoner of Law! The wind is enthralled by the fragrant rose.
The perfume is confined in the navel of the musk-deer.
The star moves towards its goal
With head bowed in surrender to a law.

The grass springs up in obedience to the law of growth:
When it abandons that, it is trodden underfoot.
To burn unceasingly is the law of the tulip,
And so, the blood leaps in its veins.
Drops of water become a sea by the law of union,
And grains of sand become a Sahara.
Since Law makes everything strong within,
Why dost thou neglect this source of strength?
O thou that art emancipated from the old Custom,[1]
Adorn thy feet once more with the same fine silver chain!
Do not complain of the hardness of the Law,
Do not transgress the statutes of Mohammed!

2. Self-control

Thy soul cares only for itself, like the camel:
It is self-conceited, self-governed, and self-willed.
Be a man, get its halter into thine hand,
That thou mayst become a pearl albeit thou art a potter's vessel.
He that does not command himself
Becomes a receiver of commands from others.
When they moulded thee of clay?
Love and fear were mingled in thy making:
Fear of this world and of the world to come, fear of death,
Fear of all the pains of earth and heaven.
Love of riches and power, love of country,

[1] The religious law of Islam.

Love of self and kindred and wife.
The mixing of clay with water nourishes the body,[2]
But he that is drowned in sin dies an evil death.
So long as thou hold'st the staff of "There is no God but He,"[3]
Thou wilt break every spell of fear.
One to whom God is as the soul in his body,
His neck is not bowed before vanity.
Fear finds no way into his bosom,
His heart is afraid of none but Allah.
Whoso dwells in the Moslem Faith

Is free from the bonds of wife and child.
He withdraws his gaze from all except God
And lays the knife to the throat of his son.[4]
Though single, he is like a host in
onset: Life is cheaper in his eyes than
wind. The profession of Faith is the
shell, but prayer is the pearl:

The Moslem's heart deems prayer a lesser pilgrimage.[5]
In the Moslem's hand prayer is like a dagger
Killing sin and forwardness and wrong.
Fasting makes an assault upon hunger and thirst
And breaches the citadel of sensuality.
The pilgrimage enlightens the minds of the Faithful:
It teaches separation from one's home and destroys attachment to one's native land.
It is an act of devotion in which all feel themselves to be
one, It binds together the leaves of the book of religion.
Almsgiving causes love of riches to pass away
And makes equality familiar.

---

[2] *I.e.* water is an indispensable element in the life of the body.
[3] The first article of the Mohammedan creed.
[4] Like Abraham when he was about to sacrifice Isaac or (as Moslems generally believe) Ishmael.
[5] The lesser pilgrimage *('umra)* is not obligatory like the greater pilgrimage *(hajj)*.

It fortifies the heart with righteousness,[6]
It increases wealth and diminishes fondness for wealth.
All this is a means of strengthening thee: Thou
art impregnable if thy Islam be strong. Draw
might from the litany "O Almighty One!" That
thou mayst ride the camel of thy body.[7]

3. Divine Vicegerency[8]

If thou canst rule thy camel, thou wilt rule the world

And wear on thine head the crown of Solomon.
Thou wilt be the glory of the world whilst the world
lasts, And thou wilt reign in the kingdom incorruptible.
'Tis sweet to be God's vicegerent in the world
And exercise sway over the elements.
God's vicegerent is as the soul of the universe,
His being is the shadow of the Greatest Name.
He knows the mysteries of part and whole,
He executes the command of Allah in the world.
When he pitches his tent in the wide world,

He rolls up this ancient carpet.[9]
His genius abounds with life and desires to manifest itself:
He will bring another world into existence.
A hundred worlds like this world of parts and wholes
Spring up, like roses, from the seed of his imagination.
He makes every raw nature ripe,
He puts the idols out of the sanctuary.

---

[6] The original quotes part of a verse in the Koran (ch. 3, v. 86), where it is said, "Ye shall never attain unto righteousness until ye give in alms of that which ye love."

[7] *I.e.* overcome the lusts of the flesh.

[8] Here Iqbal interprets in his own way the Súfí doctrine of the *Insán al-kámil* or Perfect Man, which teaches that every man is potentially a microcosm, and that when he has become spiritually perfect, all the Divine attributes are displayed by him, so that as saint or prophet he is the Godman, the representative and vicegerent of God on earth.

I.e. his appearance marks the end of an epoch.

Heartstrings give forth music at his touch,
He wakes and sleeps for God alone.
He teaches age the melody of youth
And endows everything with the radiance of youth.
To the human race he brings both a glad message and a warning,
He comes both as a soldier and as a marshal and prince.
He is the final cause of "God taught Adam the names of all things,"[10]
He is the inmost sense of "Glory to Him that transported His servant by night."[11]
His white hand is strengthened by the staff,[12]
His knowledge is twinned with the power of a perfect man.
When that bold cavalier seizes the reins,
The steed of Time gallops faster.
His awful mien makes the Red Sea dry,
He leads Israel out of Egypt.
At his cry, "Arise," the dead spirits
Rise in their bodily tomb, like pines in the field.
His person is an atonement for all the world,

By his grandeur the world is saved. [13]
His protecting shadow makes the mote familiar with the sun,
His rich substance makes precious all that exists.
He bestows life by miraculous works, He
founds a new system to work by. Splendid
visions rise from the print of his foot, Many a
Moses is entranced by his Sinai.
He gives a new explanation of Life, A
new interpretation of this dream. His
hidden being is Life's mystery, The
Nature travails in blood for generations
To compose the harmony of his personality.

[10] Koran, ch. 2, v. 29. The Ideal Man is the final cause of creation.
[11] Koran, ch. 17, v. 1, referring to the Ascension of the Prophet.
[12] For the white hand (of Moses) cf. Koran, ch. 7, v. 105, ch. 26, v. 32, and Exodus, ch. 4, v. 6.
[13] These four lines may allude to Jesus, regarded as a type of the Perfect Man.

When our handful of earth has reached the zenith,
That champion will come forth from this dust!
There sleeps amidst the ashes of To-day
The flame of a world-consuming morrow.
Our bud enfolds a garden of roses,
Our eyes are bright with to-morrow's dawn.
Appear, O rider of Destiny!
Appear, O light of the dark realm of Change!
Illumine the scene of existence,
Dwell in the blackness of our eyes!
Silence the noise of the nations,
Imparadise our ears with thy music!
Arise and tune the harp of brotherhood,
Give us back the cup of the wine of love!
Bring once more days of peace to the world,
Give a message of peace to them that seek battle!

Mankind are the cornfield and thou the harvest,
hou art the goal of Life's caravan.
The leaves are scattered by Autumn's fury:
Oh, do thou pass over our gardens as the Spring!
Receive from our downcast brows
The homage of little children and of young men and old!
When thou art there, we will lift up our heads,
Content to suffer the burning fire of this world.

10. Setting Forth The Inner Meanings Of The Names Of Ali

SETTING FORTH THE INNER MEANINGS OF THE NAMES OF ALI

Ali is the first Moslem and the King of men,
In Love's eyes Ali is the treasure of the Faith.
Devotion to his family inspires me with life
So that I am as a shining pearl.
Like the narcissus, I am enraptured with gazing.
Like perfume, I am straying through his pleasure-garden.
If holy water gushes from my earth, he is the source.

If wine pours from my grapes, he is the cause.
I am dust, but his sun hath made me as a mirror:
Song can be seen in my breast.
From Ali's face the Prophet drew a fair omen,
By his majesty the true religion is glorified.
His commandments are the strength of Islam:
All things pay allegiance to his House.
The Apostle of God gave him the name Bú Turáb;
God in the Koran called him "the Hand of Allah.
" Every one that is acquainted with Life's mysteries

Knows what is the inner meaning of the names of Ali.
The dark clay, whose name is the body Our reason is
ever bemoaning its iniquity.

On account of it our sky-reaching thought plods o'er the earth;
It makes our eyes blind and our ears deaf.
It hath in its hand a two-edged sword of lust:
Travellers' hearts are broken by this brigand.
Ali, the Lion of God, subdued the body's clay
And transmuted this dark earth to gold.
Murtazá, by whose sword the splendour of Truth was revealed,

Is named Bú Turáb from his conquest of the
body.[1] Man wins territory by prowess in battle,
But his brightest jewel is mastery of himself.
Whosoever in the world becomes a Bú Turáb
Turns back the sun from the west;[2]

Whosoever saddles tightly the steed of the body
Sits like the bezel on the seal of sovereignty:
Here the might of Khaibar is under his feet,[3]
And hereafter his hand will distribute
the water of Kauthar.[4]
Through self-knowledge he acts as God's Hand,
And in virtue of being God's Hand he reigns overall.
His person is the gate of the city of the sciences:
Arabia, China, and Greece are subject to him.
If thou wouldst drink clear wine from thine own grapes,
Thou must needs wield authority over thine own earth.

---

[1] Murtazá, "he whom with God is pleased," is a name of Ali. Bú Turáb means literally "father of earth."

[2] A miracle of the Prophet.

[3] The fortress of Khaibar, a village in the Hijáz, was captured by the Moslems in a.d. 628. Ali performed great feats of valour on this occasion.

[4] A river of Paradise.

To become earth is the creed of a moth.
Be a conqueror of earth; that alone is worthy of a man.
Thou art soft as a rose. Become hard as a stone,

That thou mayst be the foundation of the wall of the garden!
Build thy clay into a Man,
Build thy Man into a World!

If thou art unfit to be either a wall or a door,
Someone else will make bricks of thine earth.
O thou who complainest of the cruelty of Heaven,
Thou whose glass cries out against the injustice of the stone,
How long this wailing and crying and lamentation?
How long this perpetual beating of thy breast?
The pith of Life is contained in action,
To delight in creation is the law of Life.

Arise and create a new world!
Wrap thyself in flames, be an Abraham![5]
To comply with this ill-starred world
Is to fling away thy buckler on the field of battle.
The man of strong character who is master of himself
Will find Fortune complaisant.
If the world does not comply with his
humour, He will try the hazard of war with
Heaven; He will dig up the foundations of the
universe And cast its atoms into a new mould.
He will subvert the course of Time
And wreck the azure firmament.
By his own strength he will produce
A new world which will do his
pleasure. If one cannot live in the
world as beseems a man,

---

[5] See note on l. 213.

It is true life to give up one's soul.
He that hath sound intelligence
Will prove his strength by great enterprises.
'Tis sweet to use love in hard tasks
And, like Abraham, to gather roses from
flames.[6] The potentialities of men of action
Are displayed in willing acceptance of what is difficult.
Mean spirits have no weapon but spite,
This is their one rule of life.
But Life is power made manifest,
And its mainspring is the desire for victory.
Mercy out of season is a coldness of Life's blood,
A break in the rhythm of Life's music.
Whoever is sunk in the depths of ignominy
Calls his weakness contentment.
Weakness is the plunderer of Life,
Its womb is teeming with fears and lies.
Its soul is empty of virtues,
Its milk is a fattening for vices.
O man of sound judgement, beware!
This spoiler is lurking in ambush.
Be not his dupe, if thou art wise:
Chameleon-like, he changes colour every moment.
Even by keen observers his form is not discerned:
Veils are thrown over his face.
Now he is muffled in pity and gentleness,
Now he wears the cloak of humility.
Sometimes he is disguised as a victim of oppression,
Sometimes as one whose sins are to be excused.
He appears in the shape of self-indulgence
And robs the strong man's heart of courage.

Strength is the twin of Truth.

---

[6] The burning pyre on which Abraham was thrown lost its heat and was transformed into a rose-garden.

If thou knowest thyself, strength is the Truth-revealing glass.
Life is the seed, and power the crop:
Power explains the mystery of truth and falsehood.
The false claimant, if he be possessed of power,
Needs no argument for his claim.
Falsehood derives from power the authority of
truth, And by falsifying truth deems itself true.
Its creative word transforms poison into nectar.
It says to Good, "Thou art bad," and Good becomes Evil.
O thou that art heedless of the trust committed to thee,
Esteem thyself superior to both worlds! [7]

Gain knowledge of Life's mysteries!
Be a tyrant! Ignore all except God!

O man of understanding, open thine eyes, ears, and lips![8]
If than thou seest not the Way of Truth, laugh at me!

[7] The "trust" which God offered to Man, and which Man accepted, after it had been refused by Heaven and Earth (Koran, ch. 33, v. 72), is the divine vicegerency, *i.e.* the duty of displaying the divine attributes.
[8] A parody of the verse in the Masnaví quoted above. See l. 603.

11. Story Of A Young Man Of Merv Who Came To The Saint Ali Hujwírí...

STORY OF A YOUNG MAN OF MERV WHO CAME TO THE SAINT ALI HUJWÍRÍ—GOD HAVE MERCY ON HIM! AND COMPLAINED THAT HE WAS OPPRESSED BY HIS ENEMIES

The saint of Hujwír was venerated by the peoples,
And Pír-i Sanjar visited his tomb as a pilgrim.[1]
With ease he broke down the mountain-barriers loss
And sowed the seed of Islam in India.
The age of Omar was restored by his godliness,

The fame of the Truth was exalted by his words.
He was a guardian of the honour of the Koran,
The house of Falsehood fell in ruins at his gaze.
The dust of the Panjáb was brought to life by his breath,
Our dawn was made splendid by his sun.

[1] Hujwírí, author of the oldest Persian treatise on Sufism, was a native of Ghazna in Afghanistan. He died at Lahore about a.d. 1072. Pír-i Sanjar is the renowned saint, Mu'ínuddín, head of the Chishtí order of dervishes, who died in A. n. 1235 at Ajmír.

He was a lover, and withal a courier of Love:
The secrets of Love shone forth from his brow.
I will tell a story of his perfection
And enclose a whole rose-bed in a single bud.
A young man, cypress-tall,
Came from the town of Merv to Lahore.
He went to see the venerable saint,
That the sun might dispel his darkness. I am
hemmed in," he said, "by foes; I am as a
glass in the midst of stones.

Do thou teach me, O sire of heavenly rank?
How to lead my life amongst enemies!"
The wise Director, in whose nature
Love had allied mercy with wrath,
Answered: "Thou art unread in Life's lore,
Careless of its end and its beginning.
Be without fear of others!

Thou art a sleeping force: awake!
When the stone was anxious on account of the glass,
It became glass and got into the way of breaking.
If the traveller thinks himself weak,
He delivers his soul unto the brigand.
How long wilt thou regard thyself as water and clay?
Create from thy clay a flaming Sinai!
Why be angry with mighty men?
Why complain of enemies?
I will declare the truth: thine enemy is thy friend.

His existence crowns thee with glory.
Whosoever knows the states of the Self
Considers a powerful enemy to be a blessing from God.
To the seed of Man, the enemy is as a raincloud:
He awakens its potentialities.

If thy spirit be strong, the stones in thy way are as water:
What reeks the torrent of the ups and downs of the road?
The sword of resolution is whetted by the stones in the way
And put to proof by traversing stage after stage.
What is the use of eating and sleeping like a beast?
What is the use of being unless thou have strength in thyself?
When thou mak'st thyself strong with Self, Thou wilt destroy the world at thy pleasure.

If thou wouldst pass away, become free of Self;
If thou wouldst live, become full of Self! [2] What
is death? To become oblivious to Self.

Why imagine that it is the parting of soul and body?
Abide in Self, like Joseph!
Advance from captivity to empire!
Think of Self and be a man of action!
Be a man of God, bear mysteries within!"

I will explain the matter by means of stories,
I will open the bud by the power of my breath.
"'Tis better that a lovers' secret
Should be told by the lips of others." [3]

---

[2] These lines correct the Súfí doctrine that by means of passing away from individuality the mystic attains to everlasting life in God.

[3] *I.e.* allegorically. This verse occurs in the Masnaví.

12. Story Of The Bird That Was Faint With Thirst

STORY OF THE BIRD THAT WAS FAINT WITH THIRST

A bird was faint with thirst,
The breath in his body was heaving like waves of smoke.
He saw a diamond in the garden:
Thirst created a vision of water.
Deceived by the sun bright stone
The foolish bird fancied that it was water.
He got no moisture from the gem:
He pecked it with his beak, but it did not wet his palate.
"O thrall of vain desire," said the diamond,

"Thou hast sharpened thy greedy beak on me; But I am not a dewdrop,
I give no drink, I do not live for the sake of others.
Wouldst, thou hurt me? Thou art mad!
A life that reveals the Self is strange to thee.
My water will shiver the beaks of birds
And break the jewel of man's life."[1]
The bird won not his heart's wish from the diamond

[1] *I.e.* if he swallow a diamond, he will die.

And turned away from the sparkling stone.
Disappointment swelled in his breast,
The song in his throat became a wail.
Upon a rose-twig a drop of dew
Gleamed like the tear in a nightingale's eye:
All its glitter was owing to the sun,
It was trembling in fear of the sun

A restless sky-born star
That had stopped for a moment, from desire to be seen;
Oft deceived by bud and flower,

It had gained nothing from Life.
There it hung, ready to drop,
Like a tear on the eyelashes of a lover who hath lost his heart.
The sorely distressed bird hopped under the rosebush,
The dewdrop trickled into his mouth.
O thou that wouldst deliver thy soul from enemies,
I ask thee "Art thou a drop of water or a gem?"
When the bird melted in the fire of thirst,
It appropriated the life of another.
The drop was not solid and gem-like.
The diamond had a being, the drop had none.
Never for an instant neglect Self-preservation:

Be a diamond, not a dewdrop!
Be massive in nature, like mountains,
And bear on thy crest a hundred clouds laden with floods of
rain! Save thyself by affirmation of Self,
Compress thy quicksilver into silver ore!
Produce a melody from the string of
Self, Make manifest the secrets of Self!

13. Story Of The Diamond And The Coal

STORY OF THE DIAMOND AND THE COAL

Now I will open one more gate of Truth,
I will tell thee another tale.
The coal in the mine said to the diamond,
"O thou entrusted with splendours everlasting,
We are comrades, and our being is one;
The source of our existence is the same,
Yet while I die here in the anguish of worthlessness,
Thou art set on the crowns of emperors.

My stuff is so vile that I am valued less than earth,
Whereas the mirror's heart is rent by thy beauty.
My darkness illumines the chafing-dish,
Then my substance is incinerated at last.
Everyone puts the sole of his foot on my head
And covers my stock of existence with ashes.
My fate must needs be deplored.
Dost, thou know what is the gist of my being?
Thou art a condensed wavelet of smoke,
Endowed with the properties of a single spark.
Both in feature and nature thou art star-like,

Splendours rise from every side of thee.
Now thou becom'st the light of a monarch's eye,

Now thou adornest the haft of a dagger."
"O sagacious friend!" said the diamond,
Dark earth, when hardened, becomes in dignity as a bezel.
Having been at strife with its environment,
It is ripened by the struggle and grows hard like a stone.
'Tis this ripeness that has endowed my form with light
And filled my bosom with radiance.
Because thy being is immature, thou hast become abased.
Because thy body is soft, thou art burnt.
Be void of fear, grief, and anxiety.
Be hard as a stone, be a diamond!
Whosoever strives hard and grips tight,
The two worlds are illumined by him.
A little earth is the origin of the Black Stone

Which puts forth its head in the Ka'ba:
Its rank is higher than Sinai,
It is kissed by the swarthy and the fair. In
solidity consists of the glory of Life;
Weakness is worthlessness and
immaturity."

14. Story Of The Sheikh And The Brahmin, Followed By A Conversation...

STORY OF THE SHEIKH AND THE BRAHMIN, FOLLOWED BY A CONVERSATION BETWEEN GANGES AND HIMALAYA TO THE EFFECT THAT THE CONTINUATION OF SOCIAL LIFE DEPENDS ON FIRM ATTACHMENT TO THE CHARACTERISTIC TRADITIONS OF THE COMMUNITY

At Benares lived a venerable Brahmin,
Whose head was deep in the ocean of Being and Not-being.
He had a large knowledge of philosophy
But was well-disposed to the seekers after God.
His mind was eager to explore new problems,
His intellect moved on a level with the Pleiades.

His nest was as high as that of the Anká;[1]
Sun and moon were cast, like rue, on the flame of his
thought.[2] For a long time he laboured and sweated,

[1] A mysterious bird, of which nothing is known except its name.
[2] Rue-seed is burned for the purpose of fumigation.

But philosophy brought no wine to his Cup.
Although he set many a snare in the gardens of learning,
His snares never caught a glimpse of the Ideal bird.
And notwithstanding that the nails of his thought were dabbled with blood, The knot of Being and Not-being remained untied.

The sighs on his lips bore witness to his despair,
His countenance told tales of his distraction. One day he visited an excellent Sheikh,
A man who had in his breast a heart of gold.
The Sheikh laid the seal of silence on his lips
While he lent his ear to the Sage's discourse.
Then he said: "O wanderer in the lofty sky,
Pledge thyself to be true, for a little, to the earth!
Thou hast lost thy way in wildernesses of speculation,

Thy fearless thought hath passed beyond Heaven.
Be reconciled with earth, O sky-traveller!
Do not wander in quest of the essence of the stars!
I do not bid thee abandon thine idols.
Art thou an unbeliever? Then be worthy of the badge of

unbelief![3] O inheritor of ancient culture,

Turn not thy back on the path thy fathers trod!
If a people's life is derived from unity,
Unbelief too is a source of unity.
Thou that art not even a perfect infidel
Art unfit to worship at the shrine of the spirit.
We both are far astray from the road of devotion:
Thou art far from Ázar, and I from Abraham.[4]
Our Majnún hath not fallen into melancholy for his Lailá's sake:

---

[3] "The badge of unbelief": here the original has *zunnár* (ζωνάριον), *i.e.* the sacred thread worn by Zoroastrians and other non-Moslems.

[4] Ázar, the father of Abraham, was an idolater.

He hath not become perfect in the madness of love.
When the lamp of Self expires,
What is the use of heaven-surveying imagination?"
Once on a time, laying hold of the skirt of the mountain,
Ganges said to Himalaya:
"O thou mantled in snow since the morn
of creation, Thou whose form is girdled with streams,
God made thee a partner in the secrets of heaven
But deprived thy foot of graceful gait.
He took away from thee the power to walk:
What avails this sublimity and stateliness?
Life springs from perpetual movement:
Motion constitutes the wave's whole existence."
When the mountain heard this taunt from the river,
He puffed angrily like a sea of fire,

And answered: "Thy wide waters are my looking-glass;
Within my bosom are a hundred rivers like thee.

This graceful gait of thine is an instrument of death:
Whoso goeth from Self is met to die.
Thou hast no knowledge of thine own case,
Thou exultest in thy misfortune: thou art a fool!
O born of the womb of the revolving sphere,
A fallen-in bank is better than thou!
Thou hast made thine existence an offering to the ocean,
Thou hast thrown the rich purse of thy life to the highwayman.
Be self-contained like the rose in the garden,
Do not go to the florist in order to smell sweet!
To live is to grow in thyself

And gather roses from thine own flowerbed.
Ages have gone by, and my foot is fast in earth:
Dost, thou fancy that I am far from my goal.
My being grew and reached the sky,

The Pleiades sank to rest under my skirts.
Thy being vanishes in the ocean,
But on my crest the stars bow their heads.

Mine eye sees the mysteries of heaven,
Mine ear is familiar with angels' wings.
Since I glowed with the heat of unceasing toil,
I amassed rubies, diamonds, and other gems.

I am stone within, and in the stone is fire.
Water cannot pass over my fire!"
Art thou a drop of water? Do not break at thine own feet,
But endeavour to surge and wrestle with the sea.
Desire the water of a jewel, become a jewel!
Be an eardrop, adorn a beauty!
Oh, expand thyself! Move swiftly!
Be a cloud that shoots lightning and sheds a flood of rain!
Let the ocean sue for thy storms as a beggar,
Let it complain of the straightness of thy skirts!
Let it deem itself less than a wave
And glide along at thy feet!

15. Showing That The Purpose Of The Moslem's Life Is To Exalt The Word Of Allah...

SHOWING THAT THE PURPOSE OF THE MOSLEM'S LIFE IS TO EXALT THE WORD OF ALLAH, AND THAT THE JIHÁD (WAR AGAINST UNBELIEVERS), IF IT BE PROMPTED BY LAND-HUNGER, IS UNLAWFUL IN THE RELIGION OF ISLAM

Imbue thine heart with the tincture of Allah,
Give honour and glory to Love!
The Moslem's nature prevails by means of love:
The Moslem, if he be not loving, is4 an infidel.
Upon God depends his seeing and not- seeing,
His eating, drinking, and sleeping.

In his will that which God wills becomes lost
How shall a man believe this saying?"[1]
He encamps in the field of "There is no god but

[1] See Introduction, xix, note 1.

Allah"; In the world he is a witness against mankind.
His high estate is attested by the Prophet that was sent to men and Jinn
By the most truthful of witnesses.
Leave words and seek that spiritual state,
Shed the light of God o'er the darkness of works!
Albeit clad in kingly robe, live as a dervish,
Live wakeful and meditating on God!
Whatever thou doest, let it be thine aim therein to draw nigh to God,
That His glory may be made manifest by thee.

Peace becomes an evil if its object be aught else.
War is good if its object is God.
If God be not exalted by our swords,
War dishonours the people.
The holy Sheikh Miyán Mír Walí,[2]

By the light of whose soul every hidden thing was
revealed His feet were firmly planted on the path of
Mohammed, He was a flute for the impassioned music of
love. His tomb keeps our city safe from harm
And causes the beams of true religion to shine on us.
Heaven stooped its brow to his threshold,
The Emperor of India was one of his disciples.[3]
Now, this monarch had sown the seed of ambition in his heart
And was resolved on conquest.

The flames of vain desire were alight in him,
He was teaching his sword to ask, "Is there anymore?"[4]
In the Deccan was a great noise of war,
His army stood on the battlefield.
He went to the Sheikh of heaven-high dignity
That he might receive his blessing:

---

[2] A celebrated Moslem saint, who died at Lahore in a.d. 1635.

[3] Aurangzíb.

[4] Koran, ch. 50, v. 29.

The Moslem turns from this world to God
And strengthens policy with prayer.
The Sheikh made no answer to the Emperor's speech,
The assembly of dervishes was all ears,
Until a disciple, in his hand a silver coin,
Opened his lips and broke the silence,
Saying, "Accept this poor offering from me,
O guide of them that have lost the way to God!

My limbs were bathed in sweat of labour
Before I put away a dirhem in my skirt."
The Sheikh said: "This money ought to be given to our Sultan,
Who is a beggar wearing the raiment of a king.
Though he holds sway over sun, moon, and stars,
Our Emperor is the most penniless of mankind.
His eye is fixed on the table of strangers,
The fire of his hunger hath consumed a whole world.
His sword is followed by famine and plague,

His culture lays a wide land waste.
The folk are crying out because of his indigence,
His empty-headedness, and his oppression of the weak.
His power is an enemy to all:

Humankind are the caravan and he the brigand.
In his self-delusion and ignorance
He calls pillage by the name of empire.
Both the royal troops and those of the enemy
Are cloven in twain by the sword of his hunger.
The beggar's hunger consumes his own soul,

But the sultan's hunger destroys state and religion.
Whoso shall draw the sword for anything except
Allah, His sword is sheathed in his own breast."

16. Precepts Written For The Moslems Of India By Mír Naját Nakshband...

PRECEPTS WRITTEN FOR THE MOSLEMS OF INDIA BY MÍR NAJÁT NAKSHBAND, WHO IS GENERALLY KNOWN AS BÁBÁ SAHRÁ'Í

O thou that hast grown from earth, like a rose,
Thou too art born of the womb of Self.
Do not abandon Self! Persist therein!
Be a drop of water and drink up the ocean!
Glowing with the light of Self as thou art,
Make Self strong, and thou wilt endure.

Thou gett'st profit from this trade,
Thou gain'st riches by preserving this commodity.
Thou hast being, and art thou afraid of not-being?
O foolish one, thy understanding is at fault.
Since I am acquainted with the harmony of Life,
I will tell thee what is the secret of Life
To sink into thyself like the pearl,

Then to emerge from thine inward solitude.
To collect sparks beneath the ashes,
And become a flame and dazzle men's eyes.
Go, burn the house of forty years' tribulation,
Move round thyself! Be a circling flame!
What is Life but to be freed from moving round others

And to regard thyself as the Holy Temple?
Beat thy wings and escape from the attraction of Earth.
Like birds, be safe from falling.
Unless thou art a bird, thou wilt do wisely
Not to build thy nest on the top of a cave.
O thou that seekest to acquire knowledge,
I say o'er to thee the message of the Sage of
Rúm:[1] "Knowledge, if it lie on thy skin, is a snake;
Knowledge, if thou take it to heart, is a friend."
Hast, thou heard how the Master of Rúm
Gave lectures on philosophy at Aleppo?
Fast in the bonds of intellectual proofs,

Drifting o'er the dark and stormy sea of understanding;
A Moses unillumined by Love's Sinai, Ignorant of Love
and of Love's passion.
He discoursed on Scepticism and Neoplatonism
And strung many a brilliant pearl of metaphysic.
He unravelled the problems of the Peripatetics,
The light of his thought made clear whatever was obscure.
Heaps of books lay around and in front of him,
And on his lips was the key to all their mysteries.
Shams-i Tabríz, directed by Kamál,[2]
Sought his way to the college of Jaláluddín Rúmí
And cried out, "What is all this noise and babble?

---

[1] Jaláluddín Rúmí.
[2] Bábá Kamâluddín Jundí. For Shams-i Tabríz and his relation to Jaláluddín Rúmí see my *Selected Poems from the Díváni Shamsi Tabríz* (Cambridge, 1898).

What are all these syllogisms and judgements and demonstrations?" "Peace, O fool!" exclaimed the Maulavi, "Do not laugh at the doctrines of the sages.
Get thee out of my college!
This is argument and discussion: what hast thou to do with it?
My discourse is beyond thy understanding,
It will not brighten the glass of thy perception.
" These words increased the anger of Shams-i
Tabríz And caused a fire to burst forth from his
soul. The lightning of his look fell on the earth,
And the glow of his breath made the dust spring into flames.
The spiritual fire burned the intellectual stack

And clean consumed the book of philosophy.
The Maulavi, being a stranger to Love's miracles
And unversed in Love's harmonies,
Cried, "How didst thou kindle this fire,
Which hath burned the books of the philosophers?"
The Sheikh answered, "O unbelieving Moslem,
This is vision and ecstasy: what hast thou to do with it?
My state is beyond thy thought,
My flame is the Alchemist's elixir."
Thou hast drawn thy substance from the snow of philosophy,
The cloud of thy thought sheds nothing but hailstones.
Kindle a fire in thy rubble,
Foster a flame in thy earth!
The Moslem's knowledge is perfected by spiritual fervour,

The meaning of Islam is *Renounce what shall pass away.*
When Abraham escaped from the bondage of "that which
sets,"[3] He sat unhurt in the midst of flames.
Thou hast cast knowledge of God behind thee
And squandered thy religion for the sake of a loaf.

---

[3] Abraham refused to worship the sun, moon, and stars, saying, "I love not them that set" (Koran, ch. 6, v. 76).

Thou art hot in pursuit of antimony,
Thou art unaware of the blackness of thine own eye.
Seek the Fountain of Life from the sword's edge,
And the River of Paradise from the dragon's mouth,
Demand the Black Stone from the door of the house of idols,
And the musk-deer's bladder from a mad dog,

But do not seek the glow of Love from the knowledge of to-
day, Do not seek the nature of Truth from this infidel's cup!
Long have I been running to and from,
Learning the secrets of the New Knowledge:
Its gardeners have put me to the trial
And have made me intimate with their roses.
Roses! Tulips, rather, that warn one not to smell them

Like paper roses, a mirage of perfume.
Since this garden ceased to enthral me,
I have nested on the Paradisal tree.
Modern knowledge is the greatest blind
Idol-worshipping, idol-selling, idol-making!
Shackled in the prison of phenomena,
It has not overleaped the limits of the sensible.

It has fallen down in crossing the bridge of Life,
It has laid the knife to its own throat. Having
fire, it is yet cold as the tulip,
Having flame, it is yet cold as hail.
Its nature remains untouched by the glow of
Love, It is ever engaged in a joyless search.

Love is the Plato that heals the sicknesses of the
mind:[4] The mind's melancholy is cured by its lancet.
The whole world bows in adoration to Love,

---

[4] In the Masnaví Love is called "the physician of our pride and self-conceit, our Plato and our Galen."

Love is the Mahmúd that conquers the Somnath of intellect.[5]
Modern science lacks this old wine in its cup,
Its nights are not loud with passionate prayer.

Thou hast misprized thine own cypress
And deemed tall the cypress of others.
Like the reed, thou hast emptied thyself of Self
And given thine heart to the music of others.
O thou that begg'st morsels from another's table,
Wilt thou seek thine own kind in another's shop?
The Moslem's feast is burned up by the lamps of strangers,
His mosque is consumed by the Christian monastery.
When the deer fled from the sacred territory of Mecca,
The hunter's arrow pierced her side.[6]
The leaves of the rose are scattered, like its scent:
O thou that hast fled from thy Self, come back to it!

O trustee of the wisdom of the Koran,
Find thy lost unity again!
We, who keep the gate of the citadel
of Islam, Have become unbelievers by
neglecting the watchword of Islam.
The ancient Saki's bowl is shattered,
The wine-party of the Hijáz is broken
up. The Ka'ba is filled with our idols,
Infidelity mocks at our Islam.
Our Sheikh hath gambled Islam away for love of idols
And made a rosary of the *zunnár.*
Our spiritual directors owe their rank to their white
hairs And are the laughingstock of children in the street;
Their hearts bear no impress of the Faith But
house the idols of sensuality.

[5] The famous idol of Somnath was destroyed by Sultan Mahmúd of Ghazna.
[6] The pilgrims are forbidden to kill game.

Every long-haired fellow wear's the garb of a dervish
Alas for these traffickers in religion!
Day and night they are travelling about with
disciples And ignoring their religious duties.
Their eyes are without light, like the narcissus,
Their breasts devoid of spiritual wealth.
Preachers and Stiffs, all worship worldliness alike.
The prestige of the pure religion is ruined.
Our preacher fixed his eyes on the pagoda
And the mufti of the Faith sold his decision.
After this, O friends, what are we to do?
Our guide turns his face towards the wine-house.

17. Time Is A Sword

TIME IS A SWORD

Green be the pure grave of Sháfi'í,[1]
Whose vine hath cheered a whole world!
His thought plucked a star from heaven:
He named Time " a cutting sword."
How shall I say what is the secret of this sword?
All its brilliance is derived from Life.
Its owner is exalted above hope and fear,
His hand is whiter than the hand of Moses.

At one stroke thereof water gushes from the rock
And the sea becomes land from dearth of moisture.
Moses held this sword in his hand,
Therefore, he wrought more than man may contrive.
He clove the Red Sea asunder
And made its waters like dry earth.
The arm of Ali, the conqueror of Khaibar,
Drew its strength from this same sword.
The revolution of the sky is visible,
The change of day and night is perceived.
Look, O thou enthralled by Yesterday and To-morrow,

[1] Founder of one of the four great Mohammedan schools of law.

Behold another world in thine own heart!
Thou hast sown the seed of darkness in thy clay,
Thou hast imagined Time as a line:
Thy thought measures length of Time
With the measure of night and day.

Thou mak'st this line a girdle on thine infidel waist;
Thou art an advertiser of falsehood, like idols.
Thou wert the Elixir, and thou hast become a speck of dust.
Thou wert born the conscience of Truth, and thou hast become a lie!
Art thou a Moslem? Then cast off this girdle!
Be a candle to the feast of the religion of the free!
Knowing not the origin of Time,
Thou art ignorant of everlasting Life.
How long wilt thou be a thrall of night and day?
Learn the mystery of Time from the words "I have a time with
God."[2] Phenomena arise from the march of Time,

Life is a part of the contents of Time's consciousness.
The cause of Time is not the revolution of the sun:
Time is everlasting, but the sun does not last for ever.
Time is joy and sorrow, festival and fast.
Time is the secret of moonlight and sunlight.
Thou hast extended Time, like Space,
And distinguished Yesterday from To-morrow.
Thou hast fled, like a scent, from thine own garden.
Thou hast made thy prison with thine own hand.
Our Time, which has neither beginning nor end,
Blossoms from the flowerbed of our mind.
To know its root quickens the living with new life:

[2] The Prophet said, "I have a time with God of such sort that neither angel nor prophet is my peer," meaning (if we interpret his words according to the sense of this passage) that he felt himself to be timeless.

It's being is more splendid than the dawn.
Life is of Time, and Time is of Life:
"Do not abuse Time!" was the command of the
Prophet. Oh, the memory of those days when Time's
sword Was allied with the strength of our hands![3]
We sowed the seed of religion in men's hearts
And unveiled the face of Truth.
Our nails tore loose the knot of this world,
Our bowing in prayer gave blessings to the earth.
From the jar of Truth, we made rosy wine gush forth,

We charged against the ancient taverns.
O thou in whose cup is old wine,
A wine so hot that the glass is well-nigh turned to water,
Wilt thou in thy pride and arrogance and self-conceit
Taunt us with our emptiness?
Our cup, too, hath graced the symposium;
Our breast hath owned a spirit.
A new age hath been endued with our beauty
And hath risen from the dust of our feet.
Our blood hath watered God's harvest,
All worshippers of God are our debtors.
The *takbír* was our gift to the world,[4]
Ka'bas were built of our clay.
By means of us God taught the Koran, From our
hand He dispensed His bounty. Although crown
and signet have passed from us,

Do not look with contempt on our beggarliness!
In thine eyes we are good for nothing,
Thinking old thoughts, despicable.
We have honour from "There is no god but Allah,"
We are the preservers of the universe.

[3] The glorious days when Islam first set out to convert and conquer the world.
[4] The *takbír* is the cry *"Allah akbar,"* "Allah is most great."

Freed from the vexation of to-day and to-
morrow, We have pledged ourselves to love One.
We are the conscience hidden in God's heart,
We are the heirs of Moses and Aaron.
Sun and moon are still bright with our radiance,
Lightning-flashes still lurk in our cloud.
Our essence is the mirror of the Divine essence:
The Moslem's being is one of the signs of God.

18. An Invocation

AN INVOCATION

O Thou that art as the soul in the body of the universe,
Thou art our soul and thou art ever fleeing from us.
Thou breathest music into Life's lute.
Life envies Death when death is for thy sake.
Once more bring comfort to our sad hearts,
Once more dwell in our breasts!
Once more let us hear thy call to honour, Strengthen our weak love.
We are oft complaining of destiny,

Thou art of great price and we have naught.
Hide not thy fair face from the empty-handed!
Sell cheap the love of Salmán and Bilál![1]
Give us the sleepless eye and the passionate heart,
Give us again the nature of quicksilver!
Show unto us one of thy manifest signs,
That the necks of our enemies may be
bowed! Make this chaff a mountain crested
with fire, Burn with our fire all that is not God!
When the people let the clue of Unity go from their hands,
They fell into a hundred mazes.

---

[1] Salmán was a Persian, Bílál an Abyssinian. Both had been slaves and were devoted henchmen of the Prophet.

We are dispersed like stars in the world.
Though of the same family, we are strange to one another.
Bind again these scattered leaves,
Revive the law of love!
Take us back to serve thee as of old,
Commit thy cause to them that love thee!
We are travellers: give us devotion as our goal!

Give us the strong faith of Abraham!
Make us know the meaning of "There is no god,"
Make us acquainted with the mystery of "except Allah"!
I who burn like a candle for the sake of others
Teach myself to weep like the candle.
O God! a tear that is heart-enkindling,
Passionful, wrung forth by pain, peace-consuming,
May I sow in the garden, and may it grow into a fire
That washes away the firebrand from the tulip's robe!

My heart is with yestereve, my eye is on to-morrow:
Amidst the company I am alone.
"Everyone fancies he is my friend,
But my secret thoughts have not escaped from my heart."
Oh, where in the wide world is my comrade?
I am the Bush of Sinai: where is my Moses?
I am tyrannous, I have done many a wrong to myself,
I have nourished a flame in my bosom,
A flame that seized the furniture of judgement,
And cast fire on the skirt of discretion,
And lessoned with madness the reason,
And burned up the existence of knowledge:
Its blaze enthrones the sun in the sky,
And lightnings encircle it with adoration for ever.

Mine eye fell to weeping, like dew,
Since I was entrusted with that hidden fire.

I taught the candle to burn openly,
While I myself burned unseen by the world's eye.
At last flames breathed from every hair of me,
Fire dropped from the veins of my thought:
My nightingale picked up the spark-grains
And created a fire-tempered song.
Is the breast of this age without a heart?
Majnún trembles lest Lailá's howdah be empty.
It is not easy for the candle to throb alone:
Ah, is there no moth worthy of me?
How long shall I wait for one to share my grief?
How long must I search for a confidant?

O Thou whose face lends light to the moon and the stars,
Withdraw thy fire from my soul!
Take back what Thou hast put in my breast,
Remove the stabbing radiance from my mirror,
Or give me one old comrade
To be the mirror of mine all-burning love!
In the sea wave tosses side by side with wave:
Each hath a partner in its emotion.
In heaven star consorts with star,
And the bright moon lays her head on the knees of Night.
Morning touches Night's dark side,
And Today throws itself against Tomorrow.
One river loses its being in another,
A waft of air dies in perfume.
There is dancing in every nook of the wine
house, Madman dances with madman.

Howbeit in thine essence Thou art single,
Thou hast decked out for Thyself a whole world.
I am as the tulip of the field,

In the midst of a company, I am alone.
I beg of Thy grace a sympathising friend,
An adept in the mysteries of my nature,
A friend endowed with madness and wisdom,
One that knoweth not the phantom of vain things,
That I may confide my lament to his soul
And see again my face in his heart.
His image I will mould of mine own clay,
I will be to him both idol and worshipper.

LIST OF TITLES WITH ISBN NO.

ISBN	TITLE
9788194914129	1984
9789390575220	1984 & Animal Farm (2In1)
9789390575572	1984 & Animal Farm (2In1): The International Best-Selling Classics
9789390575848	35 Sonnets
9789390575329	A Clergyman's Daughter
9789390575923	A Study In Scarlet
9789390896097	A Tale Of Two Cities
9789390896837	Abide in Christ
9789390896202	Abraham Lincoln
9789390896912	Absolute Surrender
9789390896608	African American Classic Collection
9789390575305	Aldous Huxley: The Collected Works
9789390896141	An Autobiography of M. K. Gandhi
9789390575886	Animal Farm
9789390575619	Animal Farm & The Great Gatsby (2In1)
9789390575626	Animal Farm & We
9789390896158	Anna Karenina
9789390575534	Antic Hay
9789390896165	Antony & Cleopatra
9789390896172	As I Lay Dying
9789390896226	As You like it
9789390575671	At Your Command
9789390575350	Awakened Imagination
9789390575114	Be What You Wish
9789390896233	Believe In yourself
9789390896998	Best of Charles Darwin: The Origin of Species & Autobiography
9789390896684	Best Of Horror : Dracula And Frankenstein
9789390575503	Best Of Mark Twain (The Adventures of Tom Sawyer AND The Adventures of Huckleberry Finn)
9789390896769	Black History Collection
9789390575756	Brave New World, Animal Farm & 1984 (3in1)

9789390896240	Brother Karamzov
9789390575053	Bulleh Shah Poetry
9789390575725	Burmese Days
9789390896257	Bushido
9789390896066	Can't Hurt Me
9788194914112	Chanakya Neeti: With The Complete Sutras
9789390896042	Crime and Punishment
9789390575527	Crome Yellow
9789390575046	Down and Out in Paris and London
9789390896844	Dracula
9789390575442	Emersons Essays: The Complete First & Second Series (Self-Reliance & Other Essays)
9789390575749	Emma
9789390575817	Essential Tozer Collection - The Pursuit of God & The Purpose of Man
9789390896578	Fascism What It Is and How to Fight It
9789390575688	Feeling is the Secret
9789390575190	Five Lessons
9789390575954	Frankenstein
9789390575237	Franz Kafka: Collected Works
9789390575282	Franz Kafka: Short Stories
9789390575060	George Orwell Collected Works
9789390575077	George Orwell Essays
9789390575213	George Orwell Poems
9788194914150	Greatest Poetry Ever Written Vol 1
9788194914143	Greatest Poetry Ever Written Vol 1
9789390896301	Gulliver's Travel
9789390575961	Gunaho Ka Devta
9789390575893	H. P. Lovecraft Selected Stories Vol 1
9789390575978	H. P. Lovecraft Selected Stories Vol 2
9789390896059	Hamlet
9789390575022	His Last Bow: Some Reminiscences of Sherlock Holmes
9789390896134	History of Western Philosophy
9789390575121	Homage To Catalonia

9789390896219	How to develop self-confidence and Improve public Speaking
9789390896295	How to enjoy your life and your Job
9789390575633	How to own your own mind
9789390896318	How to read Human Nature
9789390896325	How to sell your way through the life
9789390896370	How to use the laws of mind
9789390896387	How to use the power of prayer
9789390896028	How to win friends & Influence People
9788194824176	How To Win Friends and Influence People
9789390896103	Humility The Beauty of Holiness
9789390896653	Imperialism the Highest Stage of Capitalism
9789390575084	In Our Time
9789390575169	In Our Time & Three Stories and Ten poems
9789390575145	James Allen: The Collected Works
9789390896189	Jesus Himself
9789390575480	Jo's Boys
9789390896394	Julius Caesar
9789390575404	Keep the Aspidistra Flying
9789390896400	Kidnapped
9789390896424	King Lear
9789390575824	Lady Susan
9789390896455	Law of Success
9789390896264	Lincoln The Unknown
9789390575565	Little Men
9789390575640	Little Women
9788194914174	Lost Horizon
9789390896462	Macbeth
9789390896929	Man Eaters of Kumaon
9789390896523	Man The Dwelling Place of God
9789390896349	Man The Dwelling Place of God
9789390575909	Mansfield Park
9788194914136	Manto Ki 25 Sarvshreshth Kahaniya
9789390896509	Marxism, Anarchism, Communism
9789390575664	Mathematical Principles of Natural Philosophy

9788194914198	Meditations
9789390575800	Mein Kampf
9789390575794	Memory How To Develop, Train, And Use It
9789390896486	Mind Power
9789390896585	Money
9789390575039	Mortal Coils
9789390575770	My Life and Work
9789390896035	Narrative of the Life of Frederick Douglass
9789390575152	Neville Goddard: The Collected Works
9789390575985	Northanger Abbey
9789390896530	Notes From Underground
9789390896547	Oliver Twist
9789390575459	On War
9789390575541	One, None and a Hundred Thousand
9789390896554	Othelo
9789390575435	Out Of This World
9789390575015	Persuasion
9789390575510	Prayer The Art Of Believing
9789390575091	Pride and Prejudice
9789390896561	Psychic Perception
9789390575381	Rabindranath Tagore - 5 Best Short Stories Vol 2
9789390575367	Rabindranath Tagore - Short Stories (Masters Collections Including The Childs Return)
9789390575374	Rabindranath Tagore 5 Best Short Stories Vol 1 (Including The Childs Return
9789390896622	Romeo & Juliet
9789390896127	Sanatana Dharma
9789390575596	Seedtime & Harvest
9789390896639	Selected Stories of Guy De Maupassant
9789390575206	Self-Reliance & Other Essays
9789390575176	Sense and Sensibility
9789390575299	Shyamchi Aai
9789390896738	Socialism Utopian and Scientific
9789390896646	Success Through a Positive Mental Attitude
9789390575428	The Adventures of Huckleberry Finn

9789390575183	The Adventures of Sherlock Holmes
9789390575343	The Adventures of Tom Sawyer
9789390896691	The Alchemy Of Happiness
9789390575862	The Art Of Public Speaking
9789390896288	The Autobiography Of Charles Darwin
9788194914181	The Best of Franz Kafka: The Metamorphosis & The Trial
9789390575008	The Call Of Cthulhu and Other Weird Tales
9789390575107	The Case-Book of Sherlock Holmes
9789390896110	The Castle Of Otranto
9789390896745	The Communist Manifesto
9789390575589	The Complete Fiction of H. P. Lovecraft
9789390575497	The Complete Works of Florence Scovel Shinn
9789390896820	The Conquest of Breard
9789390896813	The Diary of a Young Girl
9789390896332	The Diary of a Young Girl The Definitive Edition of the Worlds Most Famous Diary
9789390575701	The Great Gatsby, Animal Farm & 1984 (3In1)
9789390575312	The Greatest Works Of George Orwell (5 Books) Including 1984 & Non-Fiction
9789390575992	The Hound of Baskervilles
9789390896707	The Idiot
9789390896714	The Invisible Man
9789390575657	The Knowledge of the holy
9789390575558	The Law & the Promise
9789390896721	The Law Of Attraction
9789390896776	The Leader in you
9789390896363	The Life of Christ
9789390896196	The Man-Eating Leopard of Rudraprayag
9789390896783	The Master Key to Riches
9789390575268	The Memoirs Of Sherlock Holmes
9789390896479	The Midsummer Night's Dream
9789390575466	The Mill On The Floss
9789390896790	The Miracles of your mind
9789390896660	The Mutual Aid A Factor in Evolution
9789390896448	The Origin of Species

9789390896905	The Peter Kropotkin Anthology The Conquest of Bread & Mutual Aid A Factor of Evolution
9789390896806	The Picture of Dorian Gray
9789390896271	The Picture of Dorian Gray
9789390575275	The Power Of Awareness
9789390896356	The Power of Concentration
9788194824169	The Power of Positive Thinking
9789390575411	The Power of the Spoken Word
9788194914105	The Power Of Your Subconscious Mind
9789390896899	The Power of Your Subconscious Mind
9789390896417	The Principles of Communism
9789390575787	The Psychology Of Mans Possible Evolution
9789390896615	The Psychology of Salesmanship
9789390575732	The Pursuit of God
9789390575398	The Pursuit of Happiness
9789390896851	The Quick and Easy Way to effective Speaking
9789390575947	The Return Of Sherlock Holmes
9789390575138	The Road To Wigan Pier
9789390896981	The Root of the Righteous
9789390575855	The Science Of Being Well
9788194914167	The Science Of Getting Rich, The Science Of Being Great & The Science Of Being Well (3In1)
9789390896011	The Screwtape Letters
9789390896073	The Screwtape Letters
9789390575336	The Secret Door to Success
9789390575695	The Secret Of Imagining
9789390896868	The Secret Of Success
9789390896431	The Seven Last Words
9789390575930	The Sign of the Four
9789390896004	The Sonnets
9789390896516	The Souls of Black Folk
9789390896875	The Sound and The Fury
9789390575244	The State and Revolution
9789390896882	The Story of My Life
9789390896936	The Story Of Oriental Philosophy

9789390896752	The Strange Case of Dr. Jekyll and Mr. Hyde
9789390896943	The Tempest
9789390575916	The Valley Of Fear
9789390575879	The Wind in the willows
9789390896080	The Wind in the willows
9789390575763	Their eyes were watching gofd
9789390575831	Three Stories
9789390896950	Twelfth Night
9789390896592	Twelve Years a Slave
9789390896677	Up from Slavery
9789390896974	Value Price and Profit
9789390896967	Wake Up and Live
9789390896493	With Christ in the School of Prayer
9789390575602	Your Faith is Your Fortune
9789390575473	Your Infinite Power To Be Rich
9789390575251	Your Word is Your Wand
9789390575718	Youth
9789391316099	A Christmas Carol
9789391316105	A Doll's House
9789391316501	A Passage to India
9789391316709	A Portrait of the Artist as a Young Man
9789391316112	A Tale of Two Cities
9789391316747	A Tear and a Smile
9789391316167	Agnes Gray
9789391316174	Alice's Adventures in Wonderland
9789391316136	Anandamath
9789391316181	Anne Of Green Gables
9789391316754	Anthem
9789391316198	Around The World in 80 Days
9789391316013	As A Man Thinketh
9789391316242	Autobiography of a Yogi
9789391316266	Beyond Good and Evil
9789391316761	Bleak House
9789391316778	Chitra, a Play in One Act
9789391316310	David Copperfield

9789391316075	Demian
9789391316785	Dubliners
9789391316051	Favourite Tales from the Arabian Nights
9789391316235	Gitanjali
9789391316068	Gravity
9789391316150	Great Speeches of Abraham Lincoln
9789391316662	Guerilla Warfare
9789391316839	Kim
9789391316822	Mother
9789391316211	My Childhood
9789391316846	Nationalism
9789391316327	Oliver Twist
9789391316853	Pygmalion
9789391316334	Relativity: The Special and the General Theory
9789391316389	Scientific Healing Affirmation
9789391316341	Sons and Lovers
9789391316587	Tales from India
9789391316372	Tess of The D'Urbervilles
9789391316396	The Awakening and Selected Stories
9789391316402	The Bhagvad Gita
9789391316303	The Book of Enoch
9789391316228	The Canterville Ghost
9789391316907	The Dynamic Laws of Prosperity
9789391316006	The Great Gatsby
9789391316860	The Hungry Stones and Other Stories
9789391316433	The Idiot
9789391316440	The Importance of Being Earnest
9789391316297	The Light of Asia
9789391316914	The Madman His Parables and Poems
9789391316457	The Odyssey
9789391316921	The Picture of Dorian Gray
9789391316464	The Prince
9789391316938	The Prophet
9789391316945	The Republic
9789391316518	The Scarlet Letter

9789391316143	The Seven Laws of Teaching
9789391316525	The Story of My Experiments with Truth
9789391316532	The Tales of the Mother Goose
9789391316549	The Thirty Nine Steps
9789391316594	The Time Machine
9789391316600	The Turn of the Screw
9789391316983	The Upanishads
9789391316617	The Yellow Wallpaper
9789391316426	The Yoga Sutras of Patanjali
9789391316990	Ulysses
9789391316624	Utopia
9789391316679	Vanity Fair
9789391316020	What Is To Be Done
9789391316686	Within A Budding Grove
9789391316693	Women in Love